San Diego

A Picture Book to Remember Her By

CRESCENT BOOKS
NEW YORK

CLB 870
© 1987 Illustrations and text: Colour Library Books Ltd.,
   Guildford, Surrey, England.
Text filmsetting by Acesetters Ltd., Richmond, Surrey, England.
Printed and bound in Barcelona, Spain by Cronion, S.A.
All rights reserved.
1987 edition published by Crescent Books, distributed by Crown Publishers, Inc.
ISBN 0 517 477939
h g f e d c b a

By the time the Spanish arrived in Southern California, even the least educated of them knew that back home all roads led to Rome. In the new country it would turn out that all roads led to San Diego. Though there were more important cities at various times in Spanish California, the north-south road that reached all of them, El Camino Real, was anchored at San Diego, where it met the first transcontinental road in North America which connected San Diego with the Spanish mission at St. Augustine, Florida.

The wonderful, landlocked harbor of San Diego was first explored by Juan Rodriguez Cabrillo, a Portuguese adventurer working for the Spanish king. It was a port in a storm for him when he arrived there in the fall of 1542 and was forced to stay for nearly a week until a spell of bad weather ended. He had been ordered to go as far north as possible, and like a good sailor, he followed the coast all the way up to Oregon.

Cabrillo died the following spring at the harbor that had sheltered him, and it wasn't until 1602 that another band of Spanish explorers went north to have a look at what he had found. They may not have gone even that soon if the English explorer Sir Francis Drake hadn't been going around claiming territory and attacking Spanish ships bringing treasure from Manila.

The 1602 party named the harbor San Diego for their patron, St. James of Alcala, though they agreed that it was a nice place to visit, they decided the better harbor for the Manila ships was up the coast at Monterey. It was another 167 years before any other explorers went back to San Diego. They probably wouldn't have bothered if the Spanish hadn't been worried about the Russians who were colonizing the northern part of the coast and seemed inexorably headed for Mexico. They established a fort and a mission at San Diego, which by the time of the American Revolution was one of four in Southern California, none of which was imposing enough to put the fear of God into anybody.

The Americans arrived on the scene in 1846, and after a relatively quiet six-month war, the Stars and Stripes replaced the Mexican flag. But the people who controlled things in Washington had an impending civil war on their hands and San Diego remained the outpost it had always been, but with a slightly different accent. The American penchant for building and organizing arrived a couple of decades later in the person of Alonzo Erastus Horton, who rigged a city election and then bought city land at 21 cents an acre and began moving the center of town slightly west. The only complaint anyone heard was from Horton himself, who said he had gotten tired of handling all the money he made.

Horton's was only the first of many booms, the biggest of which followed the Santa Fe Railroad into town in 1885. When the U.S. Navy established a coaling station on Point Loma in 1907, everyone said that San Diego had gone about as far as it could go. Then, four years later, Glenn Curtis took off from North Island in a hydroplane that stayed in the air for 24 seconds more than a minute and word went out that San Diego would go very far, indeed.

But though it has one of the world's greatest natural harbors and is home to a major Navy base as well as one of the country's biggest concentrations of aircraft plants, San Diego is among America's most liveable cities. Life there is relaxed, never competing with the high mobility of the rest of Southern California, and many residents devote most of their off-the-job energy to maintaining the tropical gardens that surround their homes. The climate is legendary: sunny, dry and almost always warm. The downtown business district seems almost a part of the nearby 1400-acre Balboa Park, which was developed in 1915 as the site of the Panama-California Exposition. And as if the Park and the harbor weren't enough, neat residential streets are within an easy walk of the uncluttered business district.

Though the city has been Americanized, no other city in all of California has more authentic Old Spanish flavor than San Diego. The ruins of the 1769 Presidio, the original Spanish garrison, is a nearby neighbor to the relatively new, but strikingly authentic Spanish-Colonial Serra Museum. Neither is very far from the section known as Old San Diego, which still has the original town plaza and some of the oldest adobe houses in California. It's a wonderful place to visit, even if you're not a fan of history, because of the restaurants there.

San Diego is proud of its past and has plenty of reminders of it. But it's clearly a city with an eye on the future, a city that never seems to stop growing. But they don't let the future get in the way of today's good life in San Diego. It's a terrific place to live right now. It just keeps getting better.

The Hotel del Coronado (right) is situated on the Coronado Peninsula; which is connected to the mainland by a long sand spit, Silver Strand, and by the San Diego-Coronado Bay Bridge. Elisha Babcock wanted to build a hotel that "would be the talk of the Western world" and this dream was created in the form of the striking, red-roofed Hotel del Coronado of 1887, now a State Historical Landmark. Overleaf: quaint, beautifully landscaped Seaport Village, San Diego.

4

Avenida del Mundo (left) looked quite different in 1900, when there was no rock sea-wall or beach on the ocean side. After a fierce storm in 1905 washed most of the street away, the rock wall was built to protect both the street and the homes. The beach was formed when San Diego Bay was dredged during World War II to make it deeper and more suitable for the Navy's ships. The sand was pumped from the Silver Strand into the ocean, where the currents then carried it to the shore of Avenida del Mundo, creating one of the area's finest beaches. Overleaf: La Jolla, north of San Diego, has magnificent beaches for relaxation and water sports.

Balboa Park is one of the nation's most beautiful and versatile city parks, containing museums, art galleries, theaters, meeting rooms, a zoo and facilities for over a dozen sports. Bottom left, right, below, bottom right inset and overleaf, bottom right: Casas Del Prado. Far right inset and overleaf top right: California Tower. Overleaf left, top and bottom: two of Balboa Park's exhibition halls.

15

The aerial view of San Diego (left) shows the skyscrapers of the financial district and the small compact houses in the residential area. Overleaf right: La Jolla, whose beautiful beaches are used by both residents and vacationers. Overleaf left: aerial view of San Diego taken from over Coronado. Coronado can be reached by car in only two ways: by the San Diego-Coronado Bay Bridge, and the Silver Strand, a long narrow strip of sand that connects Coronado to the mainland. Although it is a peninsula, Coronado has the feeling of an island, being virtually surrounded by the water of San Diego Bay and the Pacific Ocean.

In the aerial view of San Diego (left) is shown the financial district surrounding Balboa Park. The top of the ornate, Spanish colonial style California Tower, rising out of Balboa Park, is in complete contrast to the concrete and glass of the modern skyscrapers.

Facing page: Seaport Village.
Above: Seaport's Mukiteo
Lighthouse is an exact
reproduction of the Mukiteo
Lighthouse situated at
Everett, Washington. Left and
top: the Embarcadero, a lively
and busy harbor. Overleaf:
views of the ghost town,
Nevada City.

Top left and overleaf left: Hotel del Coronado. This spectacular 399-room hotel was built in 1887 and overlooks the Pacific Ocean. The hotel has since been a mecca for political leaders, royalty and show business personalities. Among others, eleven U.S. presidents have been guests and it has been the setting for two full-length movies. The sweeping San Diego-Coronado Bay Bridge (left), connects San Diego with the Coronado Peninsula across the San Diego Bay. Above: Seaport Village harbor. Overleaf right: relaxing on a beach in La Jolla.

Sea World (these pages), offers a wide range of attractions, from whales, seals, sharks and dolphins to exotic birds and picturesque gardens. Above, above center and top: shows featuring Shamu, the killer whale and (far right inset) Japanese women diving for pearls.

Shamu, the killer whale (these pages), spins, rolls, dives and leaps up to 24 feet out of the water. This magnificent, 3-ton creature is one of the main attractions of Sea World. Overleaf right: cliffs overlooking the Pacific Ocean at Point Loma. Overleaf left: San Diegans relaxing and enjoying Windansea Beach.

The aerial view (right) shows part of La Jolla's 7 miles of rugged and curving coastline jutting out into the Pacific Ocean. Although officially part of San Diego, La Jolla retains its own small-town atmosphere and its own La Jolla postmark. It has an exclusive shopping center, with boutiques, import shops and gourmet restaurants. Overleaf right: the sweeping curve of the San Diego-Coronado Bay Bridge. Overleaf left: downtown San Diego.

San Diego Wild Animal Zoo (these pages and overleaf), is situated in Balboa Park. The zoo is the largest in the world, housing a large number of animals including Siberian tigers, Grant's gazelles, toucans, bears, giraffes, zebras, rhinoceros and sacred ibis.

San Diego Wild Animal Zoo has extra novelties, including a recreation of an African Kraal, a tropical American rain forest and the Gorilla Grotto. San Diego Zoo contains over 3000 animals roaming freely in surroundings resembling, as far as possible, their native homelands.

HERE HE LAY
ALL COLD
AND HARD,
THE LAST
DAMN DOG
THAT POOPED
IN MY YARD.

HOTEL

Situated in San Diego's back country is Julian. Formerly a gold mining town, Julian has been preserved much as it was and has retained its heady, free-spending flavor. The old methods of panning for gold are still demonstrated (left), and visitors can feel a little of the "gold-fever" excitement. San Diego Old Town (overleaf left) was the original site of the Mission San Diego Alcala (overleaf right), before this was moved a few miles down the road.

Far right: a busy main street in downtown San Diego. Below: part of the well-preserved old gold mining town of Julian. Above: the low, white building of the Natural History Museum, Balboa Park. Overleaf right: San Diego-Coronado Bay Bridge, joining Coronado Peninsula with the mainland at Imperial Beach. Overleaf left: aerial view of Mission Bay.

Point Loma Lighthouse (far left) was erected in 1855, on the top of Point Loma. However, its light was often obscured by cloud and it was replaced by the Coast Guard Lighthouse, on the water's edge, in 1891. Top: a flame-red sunset throws into silhouette the shapes of the palm trees at Mission Bay. Far left inset: Sutherland Reservoir, in the Cleveland National Forest. The fig tree at Moreton Bay (left) provides welcome shade from the sun for picnickers. The picturesque Singing Hills Golf Club (above) is situated in El Cajon, on the outskirts of San Diego. Overleaf right: Bird Rock. Overleaf left: Sunset Cliffs.

55

Anza-Borrego Desert State
Park covers (these pages
and overleaf) nearly half
a million acres of wild,
untamed desert. Flash
floods, erosion and the
baking heat of the sun
create twisting patterns
in the dry, sandy wastes.
The desert plants
illustrated here include:
Octillo in bloom (above),
Echinocactus and Grusoni
Cacteae (overleaf right),
and Englemann's Hedgehog
Cactus (overleaf left).
Following pages: aerial
views of San Diego.